Ripley's Believe It or Not!

Developed and produced by Ripley Publishing Ltd

This edition published and distributed by:
Mason Crest Publishers Inc.
370 Reed Road, Broomall, Pennsylvania 19008
(866) MCP-BOOK (toll free)
www.masoncrest.com

Copyright © 2004 by Ripley Entertainment Inc. This edition printed in 2010.
All rights reserved. Ripley's, Believe It or Not!, and Ripley's Believe It or Not!
are registered trademarks of Ripley Entertainment Inc.

Ripley's Believe It or Not!
Body and Mind
ISBN 978-1-4222-1532-6
Library of Congress Cataloging-in-Publication data is available

Ripley's Believe It or Not!—Complete 16 Title Series
ISBN 978-1-4222-1529-6

No part of this publication may be reproduced in whole or in part, or stored in a retrieval
system, or transmitted in any form or by any means, electronic, mechanical,
photocopying, recording, or otherwise, without written permission from the publishers.
For information regarding permission, write to VP Intellectual Property, Ripley
Entertainment Inc., Suite 188, 7576 Kingspointe Parkway, Orlando, Florida, 32819
email: publishing@ripleys.com

PUBLISHER'S NOTE
While every effort has been made to verify the accuracy of the entries in this book,
the Publishers cannot be held responsible for any errors contained in the work.
They would be glad to receive any information from readers.

WARNING
Some of the stunts and activities in this book are undertaken by experts and should not
be attempted by anyone without adequate training and supervision.

Printed in the United States of America

Ripley's Believe It or Not!

BODY & MIND

RIPLEY PUBLISHING

a Jim Pattison Company

J L12
B668ma

Body & Mind

is a collection of remarkable accounts of extraordinary physical and emotional occurrences that human beings have encountered across the globe. Read about the man who could inflate a balloon with his eye, a four-year-old chess champion, and a Chinese farmer who had a horn growing from the back of his head—all in this unforgettable book.

Lizard-man Erik Sprague, who has transformed himself to look like his favorite creatures, eats live grubs...

The Mother Touch!

Two African fertility idols, which according to local folklore could produce pregnancy in women who touch the statues, were acquired by Ripley's in 1993 and became their most popular museum exhibits ever.

When on display in Ripley's Florida office, there were 13 pregnancies in 13 months, mostly among office staff. Soon the statues became headline news and they have since toured the world twice. Over a thousand women claim to have conceived against great odds after touching them.

The statues, which stand at 5 ft (1.5 m) and weigh more than 70 lbs (32 kg), have been displayed in every Ripley museum, sometimes twice, to enable as many women as possible to touch them. In the first month of the statues being displayed in the Florida museum there was a frenzy of activity as women traveled to touch them.

Ripley's®

FERTILITY STATUES
EXHIBIT NO: 8786 AND 8747
ACQUIRED BY ROBERT RIPLEY FROM THE
IVORY COAST OF SOUTH AFRICA IN 1993

There is no rule to say where the statue must be touched in order to increase the chances of conception, but a lot of women touch the woman's baby.

Double Vision

Twins occur about once in every 75 births (every 400 for identical twins), triplets once every 7,500 births, and quadruplets once in every 620,000 births. Only three cases of nonuplets (nine babies at once) are recorded—in Australia (1971), Philadelphia, U.S.A. (1972), and Bangladesh (1977). None of the offspring survived for more than a few days. Earlier reports of decaplets (ten babies) from Spain (1924), China (1936), and Brazil (1946) are not fully substantiated.

In 2003 in England, Nicky Owen (right) gave birth to non-identical twins, having produced identical twins seven years earlier—and being an identical twin herself. Experts calculate the odds of this are 11 million to one.

One of the tallest women ever recorded was Ella Ewing of Missouri, shown here with her parents. She measured an immense 8 ft 4 in (2.5 m) tall. The tallest recorded man was Robert Wadlow (1918–40) of Alton, Illinois. He reached almost 9 ft (2.7 m) in height and was still growing when he died.

Race for Life After birth, the body increases in weight about 20 times from new baby to full-grown adult. Before birth, from fertilized egg to full-term fetus, the body increases in weight six billion times!

Tiny Survivors Premature girls born in Illinois and in England have weighed less than 10 oz (285 g) at birth, almost one-twelfth the normal birth weight—and survived.

What a Whopper! Baby Fedele, born in Italy in 1955, weighed a whopping 22 lb 8 oz (10.2 kg), three times the average birth weight.

Early Entry Normal pregnancy lasts 266 days from the time of egg fertilization to birth. In Ontario, Canada, James Gill was born after just over half this time, 128 days premature. At 2 lb 6 oz (1077 g) he was less than one-fifth the normal birth weight (about 7 lb/3.4 kg).

Twin Views In Africa, the Yoruba people respect twins, and their mother is given gifts by passers-by. However, the Tumbuka people expel the mother of twins—and father, too—to live on raw food in the forest for two months.

The Greatest In 1989 Augusta Bunge of Wisconsin, became a great-great-great-great-grandmother with the birth of baby Christopher—a span of seven generations.

Move Over Boys After 110 years of giving birth to only boys, daughter Skylar was born in 1992 to the Westerholm family of North Dakota.

Blink, Blink, Blink! Three babies are born worldwide every second.

Womb of its Own In 2003 a healthy baby was born after developing on its mother's liver, which has a rich blood supply.

At only six weeks old, Margrette Klever had hair down to her shoulders!

Little Man Gul Mohammed of India, measured in 1990, stood only 22 in (57 cm) high.

MAGNIFIQUE
Even with today's medical advances, it's not expected that a woman will bear children into old age. In Paris in the 1740s, however, it was reported that at the grand age of 90, La Belle Paule Fieschi had a son.

Probably the most unusual birth ever was in 1954 when Mrs. Boyd Braxton, at 28 years old, gave birth to triplets in different weeks! She is seen here with her six oldest children—aged 2, 3, 4 (twins), 5, and 6 years old—shortly before she was due to give birth to the third of the triplets, the first two having been born 18 days previously! This birth was the result of Mrs. Braxton having a double uterus, which meant that the first two of the triplets could be born at a separate time from the third!

Little Woman Madge Bester of South Africa stood only 26 in (65 cm) high.

Genes that Last Twin brothers John Phipps and Eli Shadrack, born in 1803 in Virginia, lived to over 107 years of age. A pair of identical female twins from St. Louis, Missouri, lived to age 104.

Towering The preserved skeleton of Englishwoman Jane Bunford (1895–1922) measured just over 7 ft (2.2 m). Zeng Jinlian (1964–82) of China would have stood taller, just over 8 ft (2.5 m), but she could not straighten her back due to severe spinal curvature.

Good Old Man In Glendale, California, in 1965, Ruth Kistler had a daughter at the age of 57. In Italy in 1994, 63-year-old Rosanna Dalla Corta had a baby boy following fertility treatment. In 2003, in Chattisgarh, India, Satyabhama Mahapatra gave birth to a baby boy at the age of 65 years!

When Salvador Quini—nicknamed "The Boy Hercules"—from Salta, Argentina, was two years old, he could lift weights that were heavier than himself!

Lizard Likeness!

Erik Sprague, an entertainer from New York State, has spent more than $21,500 in transforming his body to look like a lizard!

In 1997, Erik Sprague had a surgical procedure to split his tongue into the fork-shape that it is today.

As part of his stage act, Erik eats live grubs.

Since the age of three, Erik has loved lizards and always wanted to look like one. His body modifications began with a simple ear-piercing at the age of 18, which became the first in a series of body piercings and tattoos. Lobe stretching, tongue-splitting, teeth-filing, Teflon® implants in his brow, and more body piercings were all part of the transfiguration process for lizard-mad Erik. Erik began touring with an entertainment show in 1999. His act includes eating fire, lying on a bed of nails, swallowing swords, and shooting darts from his nose. It was while traveling with the show that he met his partner Meghan, with whom he now lives in Austin, Texas. Erik's next ambition is to have a tail implant!

IN A BIND

As recently as the early 20th century, foot-binding was practiced in China mainly by upper-class women, especially of the Han dynasty. In one common method the toes were curled over and down under the ball of the foot, and strapped by bandages around the ankle, to create an exaggerated arch to the whole sole to bring the toes and ball close to the heel. The result, known as "lily" or "lotus" feet, was deemed attractive and symbolic of wealth and breeding. The deformity, however, made normal walking almost impossible, so wealthy women with bound feet were usually carried from place to place in a chair or reclining on a bed.

Staple Diet To lose weight, some people have tried stomach stapling to reduce gastric capacity and achieve a feeling of fullness with less food.

Circular plates fitted into the lower lip, to force its extension forward from teeth and gums are considered a decorative body adornment in parts of Africa. The plates are normally worn for ceremonial purposes and can be removed, although they leave the lower lip somewhat floppy. Some lip plates, which are made from wood or clay and often decorated in local patterns with plant sap pigments, are more than 12 in (30 cm) across.

Ripley's——®

LIP PLATES
EXHIBIT NO: 22592
WAX HEAD OF AFRICAN "UBANGI" WOMAN IN CHAD, AFRICA, WEARING CEREMONIAL LIP PLATE

Power Points Sharpened teeth can be signs of hunting prowess, seniority, or status within a group in several parts of Asia and Africa. The teeth are usually chipped into points using stone or hardwood "chisels."

Super Slimmer Determined dieter, Dolly Wagner of London, England, lost 287 lb (130 kg) over 20 months from 1971 to 1973.

Desperate Measures People have considered almost every procedure to help them lose weight, from removing body fat by liposuction to having their jaws wired together, which limits food intake.

Space Race Wilfred Hardy from England has about 96 percent body coverage, including tattoos on his tongue, gums, and even the insides of his cheeks.

"*25 rings and 18 in long*"

Risking Their Necks

For centuries, women (and occasionally men) in several parts of Africa and Asia have practiced neck extension. The Paduang and Kareni people of Myanmar (Burma) have achieved total neck lengths of 18 in (40 cm). At an early age, five rings are placed around a Paduang girl's neck. A ring is then added annually until the total number of rings reaches 25! These brass rings, which appear to stretch the neck, are worn for life and only removed if a woman commits adultery. Over such a long period of time, the muscles in the neck weaken and can no longer support the woman's head without the brass rings, which means that she can suffocate as the neck collapses if the rings are removed.

Despite appearance, the brass rings do not actually stretch the neck. Instead they push the shoulders down by weight and pressure.

LOSING HIS TITLE

During a 16-month slimming spell in a hospital, Jon Minnoch, then the world's heaviest man, lost an estimated 926 lb (420 kg). Most of this was fluid accumulation due to heart failure.

Tinted Lady "Krystyne Kolorful," a Canadian stage artist, has 95 percent coverage of colorful tattoos.

Instant Diet One liposuction procedure is performed almost every hour in the U.S.A. It is probably the most common procedure in cosmetic surgery and involves fatty or lipid tissue being "dissolved" and removed by suction or scraping, as an "instant" form of weight loss.

A Plate of Parasites Some radical dieters have tried swallowing gut parasites such as tapeworms and roundworms, to reduce their appetite for food.

Unemployed Calcuttan, Murari Aditya, has not cut his fingernails since 1962! The length of all of his nails together is 10 ft 5 in (3.2 m)!

File This Fingernails grow almost four times faster than toenails.

Twenty-year Artwork Rusty Field from England has about 85 percent of his body covered with 2,500 tattoo designs completed over 20 years.

Who's Counting? Bernard Moeller from America has more than 14,000 tattoos.

Ancient Tattoos The world's oldest preserved human, "Otzi" from the European Alps, is dated to about 5,300 years ago. He has various tattoos including stripes on one ankle, a cross behind the knee and parallel lines across his lower back.

Splash! Approximately two-thirds of an average person's body weight is made up of water.

Isobel Varley of Britain is reputed to be the world's most tattooed woman, as well as sporting 49 body piercings.

Turkish architect, Mohammed Rashid charges $5 to anyone who wants to take a photo of his 5-ft 2-in (1.6-m) long moustache!

Indian Sardar Pishora Singh has been growing his 4-in (9-cm) eyebrow hair since 1995!

This Indian holy man, attending the Ambubachi festival in Guwahati, India, has hair that is over 15 ft (4.06 m) long!

HAIR RAISING

- When your hair stands on end, this is a defensive biological reaction which is meant to make you look taller!

- On average, a man's beard would grow to a length of 30 ft (9 m)—if he never trimmed or shaved it in his lifetime!

- Transplanted hair takes about three months to start growing again

- A single strand of hair can help forensic scientists find out a person's age, gender, and race

Al Elderkin of Wrights Pen, England, did not wash, undress, or remove his hat for 40 years! His hair grew through the brim and crown of his tattered hat.

Maud Williams of Oakland, California, had red hair 6 ft 6 in (2 m) long in 1938.

Hair We Go! The body sheds and regrows about 100 scalp hairs and five eyelashes daily.

Hair Miles If all the hair grown all over the body in one year was added together it would measure more than 12 mi (20 km) in length.

Long Stories Many people have had unusual scalp hair growth, with lengths in excess of 16 ft (5 m). Beard hairs can grow just as long. Norwegian Hans Langseth's beard was 17 ft (5 m) when he died in 1927.

Thick and Thin Fair or blonde people have about 130,000 scalp hairs. This number reduces to 110,000 for brown hair, nearer to 100,000 for black hair, and 90,000 for red or ginger hair.

Grace Gilbert traveled with the Ringling Brothers and Barnum and Bailey circus at the turn of the 20th century.

Astrologer Shibsankar Bharati has been growing his beard for over 20 years achieving a total length of 6.5 ft (2 m).

Pictured in 1907, when Grace Gilbert was 32 years old and 5 ft 9 in (1 m 8 cm) tall, her beard was 10 in (25 cm) long!

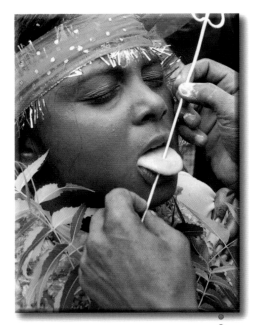

As proof of devotion to the local Hindu religion, Tamil devotees have sharp spears pushed through their cheeks, tongues, or other parts of their body.

Alex Lambrecht of Belgium has more than 140 piercings, which he performed himself! When all the rings, studs, and other adornments are installed, they weigh more than 1 lb (0.5 kg).

Expensive Adjustments

American Cindy Jackson underwent 27 cosmetic procedures in ten years, costing almost $100,000. Her operations included three facelifts, breast reduction then augmentation, and even knee alteration.

Tall Order The desire to be taller can rival that of being slimmer. In many cases, a height increase of between 2 and 4 in (5 and 10 cm) is possible. The procedure involves operations to implant bones into the shin and thigh, with surgery to muscles, tendons, and ligaments.

Rising Fees The cost of height-increase operations varies from country to country, but is about $75,000 in the U.S.A.

"spent 27 years of his life in his bedroom"

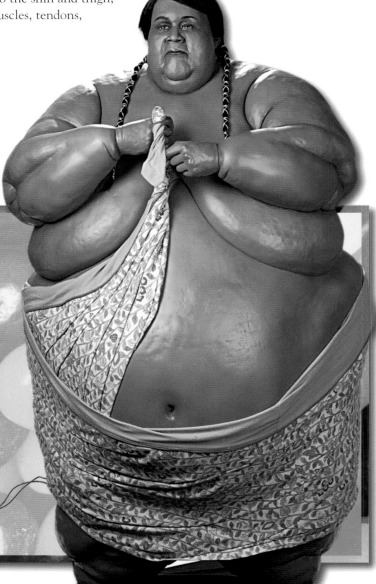

Heavy Sentence

Walter Hudson of New York, weighed over 1,400 lb (635 kg) in 1987. Hudson lived on an average daily diet of two boxes of sausages, 1 lb (0.5 kg) of bacon, 12 eggs, one loaf of bread, four hamburgers, four cheeseburgers, eight portions of fries, three ham steaks, two chickens, four baked potatoes, four sweet potatoes, and four heads of broccoli. He drank an average of 6 quarts (6 l) of soda with every meal. Hudson spent 27 years of his life in his bedroom and then became famous when he fell in a doorway. It took eight firefighters three hours to rescue him. With the help of American comedian Dick Gregory, Hudson lost 600 lb (272 kg) and began a mail-order business selling clothes for extra-large women. Hudson weighed 1,025 lb (465 kg) when he died in 1991.

Ripley's®

WALTER HUDSON
EXHIBIT NO: 1447
WAX FIGURE SHOWING THE WEIGHT OF THE ONCE HEAVIEST MAN, WALTER HUDSON

John Kamikaze suspended by eight meat hooks, re-enacting a scene from The Water Babies at the Body Craze Event!

Body Craze

The tensile strength of human skin provided a shocking display in a series of performances at Selfridges department store in London.

As the largest and heaviest organ in the human body, skin can be extremely tough and can cope with considerable strain. Performer John Kamikaze and his partner, Helmut, tested this at the Body Craze event held in May 2003 at Selfridges department store in London. Visitors were able to peer through portholes in the shop window and watch them as they performed such feats as swimming through glass shards and suspending themselves from the ceiling by meat hooks pierced through their skin.

For an episode of the Ripley's TV show, Rick Maisel fitted his

A farmer from Manchuria, China, called Wang had a 13-in (33-cm) horn growing from the back of his head.

Larry Gomez was born with a severe condition that causes hair to grow all over his face and body.

THICK-SKINNED!
In the 1920s a member of the Kalinda people of Africa suffered from keloids, which is an overgrowth of scar tissue. As he tried to cut out each thickened skin patch, another scar formed over the wounds. He reportedly ended up with 0.7-in (2-cm) thick skin that looked like a rhino's hide.

Pascal Pinon, born 1887 in Lyon, France, photographed in 1927, aged 40.

Heavy Guy When American Jon Minnoch was rushed to a hospital in 1978, his weight was estimated at 1,389 lb (630 kg). In comparison, giant sumo wrestling champion Emanuel Yarborough weighs 772 lb (350 kg).

Ms Heavyweight One of the heaviest women on record was American Rosalie Bradford who, in 1987, reached a peak weight of about 1,200 lb (544 kg).

Microscopic View The human body consists of at least 50 million million cells. About 3,000 million cells die and are replaced every minute.

Living Lens The eye lens is the only internal part of the body that grows continually throughout life.

Piercing Smile As a symbol of great beauty, the teeth of young women in the Pygmy tribe of Central Africa are shaped into triangles, using a machete.

We're Flaky Dead skin flakes make up 75 percent of household dust.

Life in a Cell The life-spans for different cells in our bodies include 12 hours for a cheek lining cell or bone marrow cell, two days for a stomach lining cell, two weeks for a white blood cell, one month for a skin cell, three months for a red blood cell, 18 months for a liver cell, and almost the body's entire lifetime for a nerve cell.

Tooth Puller Arpad Nick from Hungary pulled a 36-ton Boeing 737 a distance of 33 ft (10 m) using his teeth!

Far Sighted The human eye has the ability to see a lit match from 50 mi (80 km) away on a clear, moonless night, if viewed from a high level such as a mountain peak. Wakes left by ships are visible to astronauts as they orbit the Earth.

Vast Vessels The human body consists of 60,000 mi (96,500 km) of blood vessels, enabling blood to reach every part of the body.

MOVING PARTS

There are some 640 skeletal muscles in the body, with more than 100 in the head, face and neck. It takes:

- 6 to move an eyeball
- 20 to purse the lips for a kiss
- 25 to smile
- 30 to twist a foot inward
- 35 to twist a foot outward
- 45 to frown
- 50 to take a step forward
- 75 to speak

Queen Marguerite de Valois (1552–1615) of Navenne had pockets in the lining of her voluminous skirt so that she could carry the hearts of her 34 successive sweethearts with her at all times! Each was embalmed and sealed in a separate box!

Mouthful of Teeth!

Most humans will have 52 teeth in their lifetime—22 in the milk or baby set and 30 in the adult set. However, cases of three sets have been known, including those of Antonio Jose Herrera of New Mexico. At the age of 10 all his existing teeth were kicked out by a horse, but a new set grew in naturally. In 1896 a French doctor reported a patient who grew a fourth set, known as "Lison's case." Dr Slave lost his normal second teeth at about 80 years of age, then five years later another set appeared, which he retained until his death at 100. At the other end of the age scale, Sean Keaney was born in England in 1990 with 12 teeth.

An Eye for Color A typical person blinks over 300 million times in a lifetime, and can distinguish more than seven million different colors, including over 500 shades of gray.

High Society Air pressure falls the higher you go. So people who live in mountainous regions such as the Andes have adapted over time to survive such conditions. They have shorter arms and legs than average, so that their blood travels shorter distances, and they have over-sized lungs to cope with the lower air pressure.

In the Blink of an Eye On average, you blink 25 times each minute! So in a year, you might blink 13,140,000 times!

Digital Surplus In 1921 an autopsy on a baby boy in London, England recorded that he had 14 fingers and 15 toes.

Bloody Amazing! At any moment, about three-quarters of the body's blood is in the veins, and only one-twentieth is in the capillaries, the tiniest vessels where oxygen and nutrients pass into the tissues.

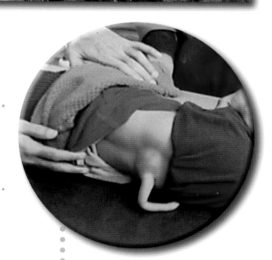

A child named Babaji is being worshiped by his community because, unbelievably, he was born with a tail.

This Spanish family display their two-, three- and, four-fingered hands!

"you blink about 300,000,000 times in a lifetime"

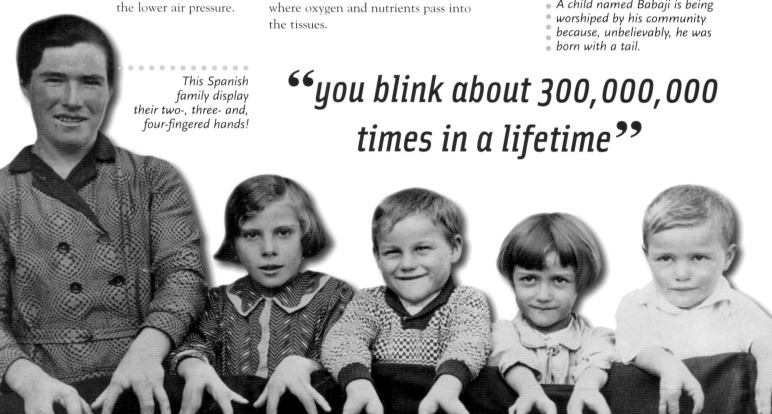

Two-toed In Africa, among the Kalanga people of the Kalahari Desert and the Wadomo people of Zambezi, there are people with two toes per foot.

Brainy A typical human brain weighs 49 to 53 oz (1,400 to 1,500 g). The brain of eminent 18th-century French scientist Baron Georges Cuvier weighed 64 oz (1,810 g), one of the largest normal brains on record.

Ripley's ®
SHRUNKEN HEAD
EXHIBIT NO: 5065
FROM THE JIVARO INDIANS OF
ECUADOR, SOUTH AMERICA

Long Liver The liver can continue to work even after 80 percent of it has been removed, and will return to its former size within a couple of months!

Painless There is no feeling in the human brain, only in the membrane surrounding it, which contains veins, arteries, and nerves. So a person would feel no pain from an injury to the brain alone.

Swallow About 0.5 pt of saliva is produced daily, and most of this water is taken back into the body in the intestines. In fact, some 8.5 pt (4 l) of combined salivary and digestive juices are produced daily, but only 3.3 fl oz (100 ml) are lost from the digestive system.

Water Everywhere The human body is two-thirds water, with most (about half) being held in the 640 muscles. Even bones are made up of one-fifth water.

A Second Look About one person in 200 has two different-colored eyes.

Three-letter Bits Ten human body parts are only three letters long: leg, arm, ear, lip, gum, rib, jaw, eye, toe, and hip!

Shedding Fast Outer human skin cells are shed and regrown about once every 27 days! Therefore humans may have grown a complete new skin about 1,000 times during their life.

Stop...Sneeze! The heart and all bodily functions momentarily stop when a person sneezes!

It is possible to make over 1,000 different facial expressions and participants took this to extremes at a Ripley contest in Atlantic City.

LIVE EXHIBIT

In 1822 French Canadian Alexis St. Martin was shot in the side. Dr. William Beaumont treated him, but St. Martin still had a 1-in (2.5 cm) hole in his stomach. For some time after, Beaumont used St. Martin's opening to study the stomach, but St. Martin ran away and, despite the hole, lived until he was 82 years old.

TOP FIVE
EXTREME LENGTHS

Straightened out and joined together, these parts of your body would be this long:

1 Nerves including micro-nerves—99,422 mi (160,000 km) (almost halfway to the Moon)

2 Blood vessels—49,711 mi (80,000 km) (twice around the Earth)

3 Tiny tubes of the filter units (nephrons) in the kidneys—over 62 mi (100 km)

4 Sweat gland tubules—31 mi (50 km)

5 Semiferous (sperm-making) tubes in the testes—722 ft (220 m)

Human Pincushion

An abnormality of nerve development means some people feel little or no pain. A few of these people make a living as "Human Pincushions."

Paddy Davidson can spear his cheeks, neck, hands, and feet with nails or skewers. Lauren Oblondo could push a metal pin in through the back of his hand, up inside his forearm and out through his elbow. "Gladys the Impaler" could push a large pin through both her thighs and then balance on it between two chairs. However, such perfomers usually take great care to keep their equipment sterile, and to know the paths of major arteries and veins, otherwise they could suffer serious wounds and bleeding.

Some people are born with unusually flexible joints, and with practice make them even more supple. The "human owl," Martin Joe Laurello, could twist his neck 180° to look backwards with his body facing forwards.

HEALTHY KISSING

Some Chinese scientists have suggested that kissing can prolong your life. A newspaper report in 1992 stated that kissing is good for your teeth, and burns off up to three calories per kiss—great news for dieters! Other researchers have suggested the opposite—that, in fact, kissing speeds up your pulse, and so increases, pressure on the heart.

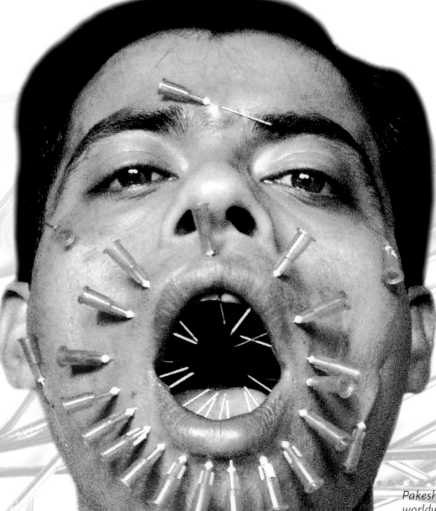

Pakesh Talukdar from India has achieved worldwide fame for such feats as piercing 24 needles into his face and eating bricks.

Finger Press In 1992 Paul Lynch did 124 push-ups supported at his front end by just one finger. Paddy Doyle did 1.5 million push-ups in one year (1988–89), an average of 170 per hour.

Legs to Contend With Queen Mary's Hospital in London is world-famous for treating physical disabilities, and especially fitting prosthetic limbs. In its soccer line-up, every player has only one leg, and the goalkeeper has one arm.

DON'T LOOK DOWN
At Acapulco, Mexico, people high-dive from rock platforms over 82 ft (25 m) high into water less than 13 ft (4 m) deep. But in France Olivier Favre dived from a board 177 ft (54 m) high, and in Switzerland Harry Froboess jumped an amazing 393 ft (120 m) into a lake—from the ill-fated airship *Hindenburg*.

Don't Sneeze "Girners" pull extraordinary faces. J. T. Saylors could cover his nose with his lower lip and chin. Bert Swallowcot went further covering his eyebrows with his lower lip!

No Spare Tire Gary Windebank balanced a pile of 96 car tires weighing over 1322 lbs (600 kg).

Running Back In 1994 Timothy Badyana ran a marathon in 3 hours 53 minutes—backwards.

Wrong Footed In 1995 Amresh Kumar Jha stood on one foot (not being allowed to touch anything with the other foot) for over 71 hours.

Month in a Tub In 1992 Rob Colley lived for 42 days in a 150-gal (700-l) barrel on top of a 43-ft (13-m) pole.

Come Again Stephen Woodmore of Kent, England, can speak at a rate of over 637 words a minute!

Twenty-one-year-old "wonder woman" Puangphaka Songskri lies on a bed of nails while a colleague breaks cinderblocks on her chest, at the set of a local TV show in Bangkok in September, 2002.

WHO SAYS MOZART ISN'T GROOVY?
Using clues from the shape, construction, and length of the grooves, Dr. Arthur Lintgen is able to name any classical record by just looking at the grooves!

Reverend Kevin Fast of Ontario, Canada, pulled two firetrucks with a combined weight of 16 tons, a distance of 100 ft (30 m). The feat was performed for the Ripley's television show in November 1999 outside the Ripley museum in St. Augustine, Florida.

"Look, No Hands!"

Welsh builder John Evans is able to balance large, heavy objects on his head. He has appeared at numerous events balancing such items as a car on his head for two minutes and 84 milk crates weighing 275 lbs (124 kg) for 10 seconds. His other balancing acts included balancing two women who weighed 210 lbs (95 kg) each and a succession of 92 people for at least 10 seconds each.

He has also been known to balance bricks, barrels and glasses of beer, and even a piece of wooden furniture weighing 240 lbs (109 kg)!

Bone Tired Moyne Mullin of Berkeley, California, could support all her weight on her elbows.

Tongue Tied American Dean Sheldon held a single scorpion measuring 7 in (18 cm) in his mouth for 18 seconds. He held a total of 20 scorpions in his mouth for 21 seconds in 2000.

Lift out of Order James Garry of Denver, Colorado can lift a 14 lb (6 kg) weight by using only the vacuum created by the palm of his hand.

MAKING HER POINT

Vietnamese circus entertainer Hang Thu Thi Ngyuen is so accurate with her aim that she can shoot a bow and arrow at a target as far as 16 ft 5 in (5 m) away, using only her feet, while standing on her hands and contorting her body so that it points forward. Since childhood, she has practised for three hours each day.

Alfred Langeven could puff enough air out of his tear-duct opening to play a recorder or even blow up a balloon. Jim Chicon could snort drinks up his nose and squirt them from his eye. People are able do this because the tube-like tear duct connected to the inner lower eyelid drains tears into the nose. Some people are able to use this duct in reverse, for water or air.

Mind on Target

Unlike most illusionists, Britain's Derren Brown definitely doesn't want his act to end with a bang—because he plays Russian roulette!

In 2003, Brown made history by playing Russian roulette live on television! The stunt, staged in Jersey to bypass British gun laws, saw a volunteer load a single bullet into a revolver with six numbered chambers. Brown, who claimed his only clue was listening to the volunteer's tone of voice as he counted from one to six, then fired the gun against his own head until he came to the chamber that he thought contained the bullet. He fired it into the air and saved himself from an untimely end!

Ling-Yong Kim of South Korea could solve complex math problems, such as determining indefinite integrals for Einstein's Theory of Relativity at the age of four.

Illusionist Derren Brown is able to read and control people's minds, memorize data, and even take away and create pain within people! He does all this with the "power of suggestion," working out details with a combination of observations about a person and through "reading" their reactions to statements or questions.

FANCY PHOBIAS

- **Agoraphobia—fear of wide-open spaces**
- **Aibohphobia—fear of palindromes**
- **Anemophobia—fear of wind**
- **Arachibutyrophobia—fear of peanut butter sticking to the roof of the mouth**
- **Genuphobia—fear of knees**
- **Lachanophobia—fear of vegetables**
- **Linophobia—fear of string**
- **Nephophobia—fear of clouds**
- **Pupaphobia—fear of puppets**
- **Uranophobia—fear of heaven or a similar spiritual place of respite**

Georgie Pocheptsov, born in 1992 in Pennsylvania, started painting at 17 months old! While most children his age were still using finger paints, Georgie was creating works of art showing four-headed giraffes and angels, all in bright, luminescent colors! At only six years old, Georgie started to display his work at the international Art Expo in New York, California, and Atlanta, Georgia.

Immovable Thoughts The brain is one of the few body parts that cannot carry out any movements at all, since it is devoid of muscle tissue.

HUMAN CALCULATOR

In the 18th century German Johann Dase could multiply two numbers—each of eight digits—in less than one minute, and two numbers each of 20 digits, in six minutes. You try: multiply 23,765,529 by 76,904,618 in under 60 seconds!

Keys to a Future Classical composer Frederic Chopin, born in 1810, is one of relatively few child geniuses who went on to achieve worldwide lasting fame. He performed his first international public tour of piano recitals at the age of eight.

Prayers in Hand The Chief Rabbi of Lithuania, Elijah the Gaon, could quote from more than 2,500 religious works he had committed to memory.

Stephanie Hale, from Essex, England, became the youngest national chess competitor in England—at only four years old! She even competed against international chess master Garry Kasparov in an Internet chess game in 1999.

Word Wary Verbophobia is a fear of words. So if you've read this far, you are unlikely to suffer from it, and especially from one of its variants, sesquipedalophobia—a fear of long words!

OUT OF IT

Shamans of the Belaro people in Papua New Guinea, after taking various concoctions of plant and animal juices, are said to enter trances lasting up to 48 hours in which they neither eat, drink, nor respond to stimuli such as loud noises or pinched skin.

An Answer for Everyone Professor Willi Melnikov of Moscow was said to be "relatively fluent" in more than 90 languages.

Something to Say Martha Ann Koop of Tennessee started to talk at the age of six months—about a year earlier than most children.

Seventies Rocker In 1977 Maureen Weston of England went without proper sleep for 18 days during a rocking chair marathon.

Facing His Fear The first person to fly solo across the Atlantic was U.S. aviator Charles Lindberg who completed the journey. He did so despite a mild form of acrophobia, which is a morbid fear of heights.

Pick a Card, Any Card In the 1930s Arthur Lloyd of Massachusetts, was known as the Human Card Index. His special 40-pocket jacket carried 15,000 notecards and he could locate any single card in less than five seconds.

Hypnotizing the Hypnotist Efrarl Rabovich had no interest in hypnotism or the power of the mind until he himself was selected to take part at a local event in Austria in 1921. The hypnotist found him a difficult subject and soon asked for another volunteer. Yet the next day Rabovich was suddenly able to hypnotize people.

Brain Drain For its size, the brain consumes between five and ten times more energy than other organs.

MEGA STORAGE

Weighing 3 lbs (1.4 kg) the human brain is the most complex collection of matter known in the universe. The total memory capacity of the brain is estimated at 100 trillion bits of data, which is equal to the information in 500,000 large multi-volume encyclopedias, or in computer terms, about 1,000 gigabytes!

Retiring to the Library Eminent South African general and statesman Jan Christian Smuts (1870–1950) could not read until he was 11 years old, but spent most of his old age, when memory powers normally fade, memorizing more than 5,000 different books.

Quick Study William Sidis of Massachusetts, could type out words in English and French by the age of two, and wrote an article on human anatomy at the age of five.

Empowering the Mind!

Dominic O'Brien has overcome childhood dyslexia and Attention Deficit Hyperactivity Disorder (ADHD) to win the World Memory Championships eight times! As a child, he suffered from dyslexia, which led to a difficulty with reading and consistent concentration-lapses throughout his school career. Over 14 years of disciplined training has helped him to correct the "imbalance" that he believes is responsible for these disorders. Along with a colleague, Dominic has used his knowledge of dyslexia and thorough research into the brain and developed the Brainwave Conditioning System, to help others suffering from dyslexia and ADHD.

In 2002, in front of a panel of judges, Dominic O'Brien memorized 54 packs of shuffled cards in 12 hours. He then took over four hours to recite all 2,808 cards, with only eight errors!

Hole in the Head!

Cutting or drilling holes into the head, known as trepanation, was practiced on almost every continent in ancient times. It was probably used to let out "evil spirits" from the brain, conditions that we now know as epilepsy, mental illness, or migraines.

Heather Perry from Gloucestershire, England, journeyed to the U.S.A. in order to undergo trepanation, to cure her chronic fatigue and depression.

Ancient trepanation used sharp knives of flint, obsidian (a black, glassy rock) and bronze, and a hand-cranked rotary drill resembling an old-fashioned carpenter's brace-and-bit. Some preserved skulls have four or five holes, often larger than eye sockets. In many cases the bone shows signs of healing, which means the subjects survived. Trepanation is still carried out in some parts of the world today. People use it to create blood flow to the brain for stimulating mental awareness, relieve stress, and as a cure for complaints such as chronic depression.

In 1990, Charles Osborne of Iowa, finally stopped hiccuping after 58 years. Despite the hiccups, he had managed to live a near-normal life and had eight children.

In Moscow, Russia, a clinic treats patients using bee sting therapy. Bee venom has been used for centuries to treat arthritis, skin diseases, and back pain. It is used today as a treatment for multiple sclerosis.

OLD NOSE JOB

In ancient India, petty criminals were often punished by cutting off their noses. To repair the wound doctors developed a method of slicing a triangular flap of skin from the forehead leaving a "stalk" at the bridge of the nose, then folding it over and down with a twist to keep the skin side outwards, and stitching it to a nose-shaped prosthesis of polished wood. A low-fronted turban hid the forehead scar.

A Mouthful False teeth have been found in remains of Romans more than 2,000 years old. Most were made of hardwood or metal but some are ivory, carved from elephants tusks. Even earlier, the Etruscans made removable dentures of gold.

As an antidote for stress at work, a company in the U.K. installed a grass lawn in their office, thinking it would have a calming effect and that it would promote relaxation while at work!

Looking Back The ancient Romans used many medical instruments that are strikingly similar to today's tools, such as the rectal speculum—for holding open the "back passage" to look up the large bowel.

Organic Painkiller Some 2,350 years ago Greek physician and "Father of Medicine" Hippocrates advised chewing willow bark to relieve pain. It worked. Much later the active ingredient was isolated and launched as a pain-relieving pill—what we now call aspirin.

Four-day Operation In 1951 Gertrude Levandowski underwent a 96-hour operation in Chicago to remove an ovarian cyst.

Self Help Ira Kahn of Lebanon removed his own appendix while stuck in a traffic jam. However, he was a doctor!

Lost and Found In 1997 Silvio Jimenez underwent an operation to remove tweezers left from previous surgery—47 years earlier.

At Lake Kirkpinar in Turkey, patients are treated with water serpents.

Bled Dry Bleeding the body to release "stale blood" or "foul humors" has been a common treatment through the centuries. Conditions such as jaundice were believed to result from too much blood—so doctors let it out! In the 1300s, 200 leeches were applied to Philus of Padua and he was wrapped in a wet blanket for three days while they gorged on his blood. Unsurprisingly, he died the next day.

In May 2003, Wei Shengchu had 2,003 acupuncture needles placed in his head! Acupuncture is an alternative method of treatment used to heal many health complaints, from stress and headaches to arthritis.

Coldhearted In 1987 a Norwegian fisherman fell overboard and his body became so chilled in the water his heart stopped beating for four hours. He revived when he was taken to a hospital and gradually recovered while linked to a heart-lung machine.

Blood Bath! In Chicago in 1970 Warren Jyrich who suffered from hemophilia or "bleeding disease" received 285 gal (1,080 l) of transfused blood—about 12 bathtubfuls—during a heart operation.

"Smoky," from St. Louis, Missouri, could breathe through a hole in his back and he could exhale smoke from a cigarette through it and could still breathe!

Man-sized Tumors Several operations have been performed to remove tumors weighing more than 220 lbs (100 kg), including one ovarian growth of 302 lbs (137 kg) and another fluid-filled cyst of 327 lbs (148 kg)—this is about the weight of two large adults.

NO THANKS, DOCTOR

In mid-19th century England, a remedy for dysentery was drinking powdered human bones mixed with red wine. An attempted cure for baldness was to sleep with a paste of bull's blood and semen applied to the scalp and covered with a towel. Treatment for earache included poking the ashes of a cremated mouse mixed with honey into the ear. Wine fermented with ground-up lice was given for jaundice, and tea boiled with snails was prescribed for chest infections.

Hard Headed In 1992 in Michigan, Bruce Levon had a head X-ray that revealed a bullet from a shooting that had occured nine years earlier lodged in his skull. Bruce had been unaware of it.

Smile, Please Frederic Green of California was pronounced dead at the age of 82—but in the mortuary the flashbulb of the coroner's photographer woke him up!

Maggots to the Rescue Maggots are fly grubs that thrive on dead and rotting flesh. They are now used routinely in some countries to clean wounds of infected and gangrenous tissue. About 100 "baby" maggots are bandaged onto the wound and removed two or three days later, during which time they have grown in size five times and left the wound picked clean of germs and decay.

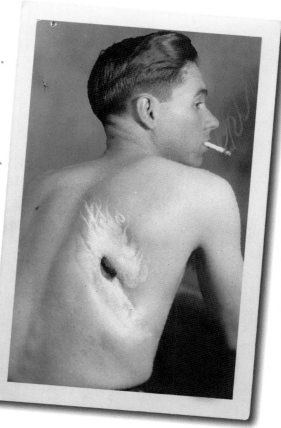

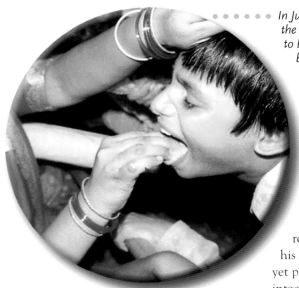

In June 2003, thousands of people flocked to the Indian city of Hyderabad in an attempt to be cured of asthma! It was believed that by swallowing a small, whole murrelfish, coated in a special herbal paste, the disease could be cured.

New Parts Norma Wickwire of the U.S.A. had eight different joints replaced between 1976 and 1989 because of rheumatoid arthritis.

Memory on Hold In 1984 Terry Wallis, aged 20, was involved in a car crash in Arkansas. It was Friday the 13th, and he went into a coma for 19 years. On Friday, June 13, 2003, Terry regained consciousness and uttered his first words. He is severely paralyzed, yet parts of his memory have survived intact for nearly two decades. He could recall events, names, and phone numbers from the time of the accident, but still believed Ronald Reagan was the U.S. president.

Scalp Invader In 1998 a woman returning from the West Indies to England complained of a severe headache. Doctors discovered and removed 91 screw-worms from deep in her scalp. Screw-worms are screw-shaped maggots of a type of blowfly that burrow through wounds into the flesh of animals and people to feed. They hatch from tiny eggs and grow to about 1 in (25 mm) long.

Bedpan Billy Munchausen's Syndrome is characterized by a desire for medical attention and treatment. In England between 1930 and 1979 William McIlroy had over 400 operations in 22 hospitals, using more than 20 assumed names. He finally gave up his visits saying "I'm sick of hospitals."

Plan Melts Away

When Monique Martinot died in 1984, her husband, Dr. Raymond Martinot, cryogenically froze her body in the hope of being able to revive her in the future. In February 2002, Dr. Martinot also died and his wishes to be frozen alongside her were carried out, in the hope that they could both live again one day. However, later that year the French court ruled that they had to be buried.

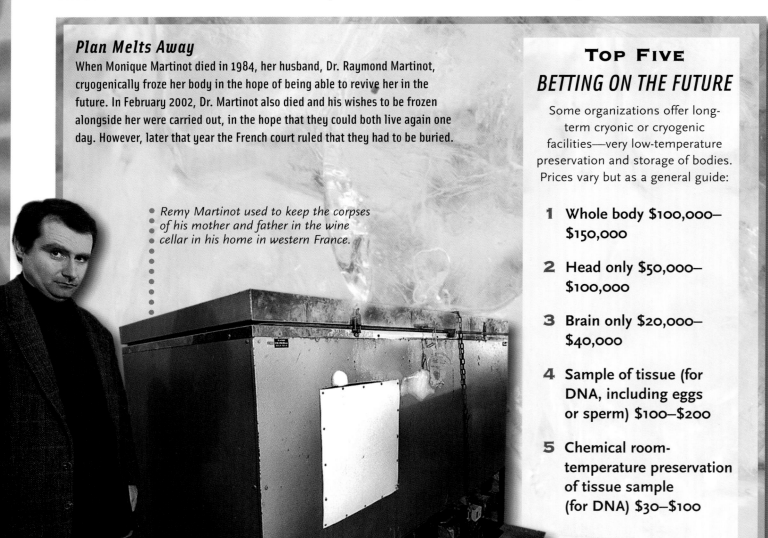

Remy Martinot used to keep the corpses of his mother and father in the wine cellar in his home in western France.

TOP FIVE
BETTING ON THE FUTURE

Some organizations offer long-term cryonic or cryogenic facilities—very low-temperature preservation and storage of bodies. Prices vary but as a general guide:

1. Whole body $100,000–$150,000

2. Head only $50,000–$100,000

3. Brain only $20,000–$40,000

4. Sample of tissue (for DNA, including eggs or sperm) $100–$200

5. Chemical room-temperature preservation of tissue sample (for DNA) $30–$100

Grave Offerings

Every year on November 2, the Day of the Dead, families in Mexico troop to cemetries to visit departed relatives, bearing not only flowers but party fare such as breads, cakes, candy, cigarettes, and alcohol.

Relatives sit around the grave and have a picnic including food such as chocolate hearses and coffins, fancy breads decorated with skulls, and sugar skeletons. It is considered good luck to be the one to find the skeleton hidden inside each loaf baked. Friends give each other gifts of sugar skeletons inscribed with a death motif of their name.

"Happy skeletons" are made in Mexico of papier maché to celebrate the festival of the Day of the Dead, which honors the deceased.

FANTASY TOMBSTONES

- **25-ton granite grand piano**
  Madge Ward, concert pianist, Texas, U.S.A.

- **Giant mobile phone headstone**
  Guy Akrish, Israel

- **Scaled-down Concorde**
  L. Spurlington, model aircraft enthusiast, South Africa

- **Giant light-bulb**
  Sal Giardino, electrician, New Jersey, U.S.A.

Dying by the Minute! About 100 people around the world die every minute.

Time's Up The most "popular" time for dying is the early hours of the morning, from about 2 a.m. to 5 a.m.—which is also the most common time for babies to be born.

Buried But Not Dead!

Following a motorbike crash in 1937, Angel Hayes was pronounced dead. Two hours before his burial he woke from his coma to the shock of his family and friends who had been in mourning for three days. So scared by his near live-burial, mechanic Hayes went on to invent and create a coffin to prevent such a horrible thing from ever happening again. The coffin he created was fitted with alarm bells and flashing lights. In case the occupant would have to wait for a long time before being rescued, supplies such as toilet paper were included. Electrodes were connected to the coffin, which in turn connected to a monitor to alert the outside world of the presence of a living person inside the coffin. To demonstrate just how efficient this invention was, Hayes actually stayed in it underground for two days and two nights!

Hayes' coffin creation was almost a home away from home—it even had food and drink inside.

Homage on High On All Saints Day in Sacatepequez, Guatemala, residents honor the dead by gathering together in their local graveyard to fly large, decorative kites.

Not Done Yet French soldier Nicola Baillot was captured at the Battle of Waterloo but freed in 1815, aged 24, when a doctor considered him close to death from tuberculosis. In fact, he survived to the grand age of 105.

No Longer Ticking Hannah Beswick of Lancashire, England, was one of many people worried about being mistakenly pronounced dead. Her will contained instructions that her body should be inspected often for signs of life, so her doctor had the body placed inside a grandfather clock to enable regular, timed examinations.

Writing on the Wall The Vietnam Veteran's Memorial in Washington, D.C., carries the names of 38 people who actually survived the war.

Unlucky 13 Author Sholom Aleichem avoided the number 13 at all costs. All his written works went from page 12 to 14. Unluckily, he died on May 13, 1916. However, his family upheld his wishes and changed his epitaph to read May 12.

Unlucky 8 American George E. Spillman of Texas was a "number 8" man—he died at 8 p.m. on August 8, 1988, aged 88.

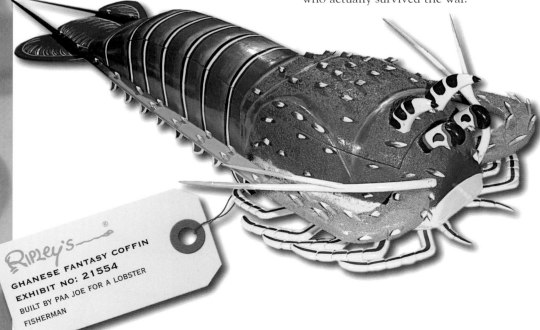

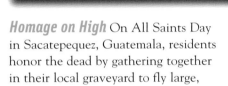

Ripley's®
GHANESE FANTASY COFFIN
EXHIBIT NO: 21554
BUILT BY PAA JOE FOR A LOBSTER
FISHERMAN

THE LIVING DEAD!

In 1960 writer Ernest Hemingway read his obituary in many newspapers after his plane had crashed in Africa. He lived for a further year. Other writers have also had premature brushes with the Grim Reaper. Rudyard Kipling stated: "The reports of my death are over exaggerated." Mark Twain made the similar remark: "The report of my death was an exaggeration." Retired funeral home director Charles Tomlinson of Florida went one better and read two of his own published obituaries, in 1995 and 1996.

A gambler named Louis Vieira and his wife were buried in Pine Grove Cemetery, Connecticut. The ace represents Vieira, the queen his wife, and the dice are just for decoration. The headstone is carved from pink granite so that the hearts on the stone cards look real.

Gruesome Memento Famous English explorer Sir Walter Raleigh was beheaded in 1618 and buried—well, most of him. His wife Elizabeth kept his preserved head in a bag for 30 years!

Uncle's Been Very Quiet . . . A local tradition in parts of Borneo was to squeeze the body of deceased into a jar and keep it in the relatives' house for a year before the "official" burial.

Last of the Great Meals In ancient Rome, Apicius, the gourmet, was so afraid of going hungry that when he became penniless, because of expenditures on his fabulous banquets, he poisoned himself.

"The sitting-room tombstone" Davis Family memorial is located in Kansas, in the middle of nowhere. It was built by John Milbert Davis, a wealthy farmer landowner, as a memorial to his wife, Sara. They were married for 50 years, but he outlived her for another 15. Most of the individual statues are of John and Sara at different stages of their lives, including John with and without a beard, and one without a hand (he lost it in an accident). This picture was taken in 1933. The tomb was not completed until John died in 1947.

TOP FIVE
IRONIC DEATHS

1 Francis Bacon, English scientist and philosopher, carried out experiments on preserving meat with snow, but caught a cold and died

2 Molière, French playwright, fell ill and died while playing the role of the hypochondriac in his work *The Imaginary Invalid*

3 Bobby Leech, U.S. daredevil, survived going over Niagara Falls in a wooden barrel, then died a few months later after slipping on a banana peel

4 Bat Masterson, legendary Dodge City, Kansas lawman survived endless feuds and gun battles to pass away quietly at his desk

5 Will Rogers, U.S. humorist, was killed in a plane crash in 1935, the newspaper column he had just completed ended with the word "death"

Sensitive Soul In 1835 French artist Baron Gros was so upset by criticism of one of his paintings, he drowned himself in 3 ft (1 m) of water.

Buttoned In Africa, a widow of the Tikarland tribe must wear two buttons from her husband's clothing—one in each nostril.

Step Out in Style

Funerals may be a sad time when loved ones are laid to rest, but some people have found a way to go out smiling—in custom-made coffins.

A coffin fit for a judge, book in hand.

A coffin in the shape of a chicken, complete with chicks!

Coffin makers in Ghana handcraft individually styled models! They come in all sorts of shapes and sizes, from animals such as eagles, cows, chickens, or crabs, to objects such as planes, boats, and luxury cars, to shoes, hoes, shovels, and even bottles! Fishermen can be buried in a fish, an athlete in a giant sneaker, a fruitseller in a papaya!

The occupant of this coffin will be flying into the afterlife in this airplane!

GHANA AIRWAYS

Mick Fowell from Norfolk, England, has an unusual coffee table in his living room—a coffin. Fortunately, it's empty!

- *Mickey had pillows and*
- *blankets and the heat from*
- *a single light bulb to keep him*
- *warm during his entombment.*

Buried Alive

Mickey Bidwell of Binghamton, New York, U.S.A. was buried alive 6 ft (1.8 m) under frozen earth for 53 days in 1932. The box in which he was buried measured 7 ft (2.1 m) long, 21 in (53 cm) wide and 24 in (61 cm) high. There was only 4 in (10 cm) clearance between the box lid and his chest. Food was lowered through an opening in the box, and visitors each paid a dime to look through the hole that also provided him with his air supply. He gained about 10 lb (4.5 kg) while underground, and spent time answering fan mail. Between 1930 and 1936, Mickey spent a total of 365 days underground!

A Great Exit Perhaps the most costly and elaborate funeral of all time was Alexander the Great's in 323 BCE. His jewel-studded hearse drawn by 64 horses traveled more than 994 mi (1,600 km) on specially-made roads from Babylon to lay him to rest in the city he had created—Alexandria, Egypt.

Year-Long Funeral The cortege of Chinese General Yi Chun traveled from Peking to Kashgar Sinklang, a distance of 2,299 mi (3,700 km). The funeral lasted exactly one year, from June 1, 1912 to his laying at rest on June 1, 1913.

Well Laid Out The elaborate funeral suit of Chinese Princess Tou Wan, who passed away over 2,000 years ago, was made from 2,000 pieces of jade sewn with gold and silk-covered wire.

Up in Smoke American Bill Johnson of California asked for his ashes to be shot into the sky as firework rockets.

Rest in Pieces Hapsburg emperors had their bodies preserved in monastery crypts in Vienna, Austria, their mummified guts in St. Stephan's Cathedral, and their hearts in the Augustiner Church.

HAVING THE LAST LAUGH

The ancient Greek soothsayer Calchas foresaw many great events, including the Trojan War. He was so amused to find out that he had outlived the hour of his death as predicted by the spirits, that he laughed until he died—literally.

Hanging Around Gene Roddenbury, the creator of *Star Trek*, arranged to send his ashes into space on a Pegasus rocket, which will circle the Earth for years.

Hard Reminder In New Guinea, when an Asmat warrior dies, his son inherits his father's skull and uses it as a pillow at night.

Silent Mourning In Australia, a widow of the Warramunga aboriginal people does not speak for a year after her partner's death and communicates in the form of gestures and expressions.

Index

Index

ACKNOWLEDGMENTS

Jacket (t/l) Mark Campbell/Rex Features

7 (t) Gary Roberts/REX, (c/l) FPL; 8 (b) Bettmann/CORBIS; 10 (b) Michael Friedel/REX; 11 (t) AFP/GETTYIMAGE, (b/l) ,Marc Alex/AFP/GETTYIMAGE, (b/r) Marc Alex/AFP/GETTYIMAGE; 12 (t/l) Joseph Barrak/AFP/GETTYIMAGE, (t/r) AFP/GETTYIMAGE, (b/l) Biju Boro/AFP/GETTYIMAGE; 13 (t/r) Deshakalyan Chowdhury/AFP/GETTYIMAGE; 14 (t/r) Uta Rademacher/AFP/GETTYIMAGE; 15 (t) Tim Rooke/REX, (c) Ripley's Believe It or Not! Archives, Sony Pictures Television (b) Ripley's Believe It or Not! Archives, Sony Pictures Television, 16 (b) FPL, (t/l) Ripley's Believe It or Not! Archives, Sony Pictures Television; 17 (c) Ripley's Believe It or Not! Archives, Sony Pictures Television, (b) Bettmann/CORBIS; 19 (b) AFP/GETTYIMAGE; 20 (t) Pornchal Kittiwongsakul AFP/GETTIMAGE; 22 (c) Courtesy of Michael Vine Associates/Nicky Johnson; 23 (t) Brownie Harris/CORBIS, (b) John Mclellen/REX; 24 (b) Greg Williams/REX; 25 (c/r) Dave Bebber/REX, (b/l) Gary Trotter/REX; 26 (t) Sipa Press/REX, (b) Nils Jorgensen/REX; 27 (t) Mark Campbell/REX; 28 (t) AFP/GETTYIMAGE, (b) Paul Coo per/REX; 29 (b) Charles and Josette Lenars/CORBIS; 30 (t) Gamma/Katz; 32 (t/l) Issouf Sanogo/AFP/GETTYIMAGE, (t/r) Issouf Sanogo/AFP/GETTYIMAGE, (b) Issouf Sanogo/AFP/GETTYIMAGE; 33 (t) Jerry Daws /REX

FPL – Fortean Picture Library

All other photos are from Corel, PhotoDisc, Digital Vision and Ripley's Entertainment Inc.